# THE FALLOW

# The Fallow

poems by Megan Neville

THP

Copyright © July 1, 2022 Megan Neville

No part of this book may be used or performed without written consent of the author, if living, except for critical articles or reviews.

Neville, Megan
1st edition

ISBN: 978-1-949487-11-4
Library of Congress Control Number: 2021951012

Interior design by Hadley Hendrix
Cover art by Erin McGean
Cover design by Joel W. Coggins
Editing by Tayve Neese and Hadley Hendrix

Trio House Press, Inc.
Ponte Vedra Beach, FL

To contact the author, send an email to tayveneese@gmail.com.

*for Marilyn Leonard*

# Table of Contents

## I

| | |
|---|---|
| Self-Portrait with Origin Myth & Orbit | 14 |
| Our Lady of Impermanence | 16 |
| To the Women Who Surrounded the Pentagon | 17 |
| Sitting On the Floor in the Dark, My Student Asks If We've Always Done This | 19 |
| & I Cringe Every Time I Hear the Word *Womb* | 21 |
| Rotational Fall | 22 |
| Legacy | 25 |
| Elegy with Apologies to Leon Jakobovits James | 26 |
| Our Lady of the Curious Exemption | 28 |
| Stand Her Ground | 29 |
| Fascinator, in Which Moving On Serves as the Eighth Sacrament | 31 |
| Ode to the Word *Vagina* | 35 |
| Our Lady of the Safe Word | 36 |
| Hands: A Cross | 37 |
| Upon First Awareness of Cloud Movement, 1985 | 38 |
| Spell to Extract Beauty from My Mother's Despair | 39 |
| Objects in the Road Mistaken for Animals | 41 |
| Digestif | 42 |

## II

| | |
|---|---|
| Elegy Toward Indifference | 46 |
| Self-Portrait as Faked Orgasms | 47 |
| Party Game | 48 |
| The Doctor Wraps Her Hand Around My Throat | 49 |

| | |
|---|---|
| On Trying to Guess My Newly-Dead Father's Computer Password | 50 |
| Morning with Empty Cat Dish | 51 |
| Our Lady of the Fallow | 53 |
| In Which I Suddenly Recall the First Plane I Saw in the Sky after 9/11 | 54 |
| Marriage Born of Caution | 56 |
| The Night My Father Died, I Almost Believed in God | 57 |
| Shelter | 59 |
| Clearing My History after Searching Plan B Availability in Utah (because no, this is not what you think) | 60 |
| Our Lady of the Restroom Stall Confessional | 61 |
| Body of Knowledge | 62 |
| Ode to My IUD | 64 |
| The Instructor Says *Breathe In*, as Though I Have Forgotten | 65 |
| On My First Case of Chub Rub | 66 |
| After All, I Promised to Read St. Augustine | 68 |
| Something In | 69 |
| Spell for Protection Against the Force You Cannot Name | 71 |
| Accidental Elegy | 73 |
| | |
| *Notes* | 77 |
| *Acknowledgements* | 81 |
| *Thank You* | 83 |
| *About the Author* | 85 |
| *About the Artist* | 87 |

***fal·low***   / ˈfalō/  *adjective*

*plowed and harrowed but left unsown for a period in order to restore its fertility as part of a crop rotation or to avoid surplus production.*

– Oxford Languages

## I.

*let the world blot  
obliterate remove so-  
called magnificence  
so-called  
almighty/fathomless and everlasting/  
treasures/*

— June Jordan

## SELF-PORTRAIT WITH ORIGIN MYTH & ORBIT

Blame gravity: Jupiter has more pull on me
        than you here inhaling my exhale, so no wonder

I am readily distracted. The moon tugs at the surface
        of water, coaxing waves to stay with her as she rolls

through her rounds. At birth a human is three-quarters
        water, & by adulthood she's wrung out to slightly

more than half. At this point I'm more tree than fetus.
        You're welcome, clouds. Out west a rock formation

pulses at the same rate as a human heart. It's spared
        the complications, the senior year breakups &

Easter morning angioplasties. As a child I collected
        stones & gave them names. Kept them in

a dollhouse, cozied into Q-tip boxes
        with Kleenex blankets. I realize now that Annie

was raw jasper, Sparkle just a hunk of concrete. But I
        loved them more than any doll. God bless my family

for humoring this. One Christmas an uncle brought
        petrified wood from the desert near his house.

It stunned me to learn how a thing existing with
        us that second could be a fossil later on but

in childhood timelines seem so finite & it hasn't sunk in
        how our present will be some future's past. He owned

a telescope & had pins in his leg from a motorcycle crash,
        took me outside to find constellations & hear how

space isn't empty: it buzzes with energy crafting
        matter to make the universe push out & away

from itself. I squint at my skin & picture atoms
        mid-spin, unaware of making me up.

## OUR LADY OF IMPERMANENCE

It's not the stones that let go, but the mortar.
Heat creeps between its particles, pushes
them apart to make room for the holy spirit.
My mother's womb decomposes in a landfill
& the house where I grew up now homes another
family. Life has scattered from the center of town.
As the spire collapses the world gasps—
memory unearthed in the release, the lack,
the unplanning. Cross my legs & toes turn blue
as all of me at the moment of my birth.
Now that we know the world will end in flame
instead of frost, I cut the inside of my cheek
on my own forked tongue again & again
& the iron of my blood tastes like home.

## TO THE WOMEN WHO SURROUNDED THE PENTAGON

with their sturdy legs, milk-flat breasts,
        & embroidered panels of muslin—

who deployed on overnight greyhounds
        leaving their children in ohio while

they took on world leaders with needles
        & thread greased with beeswax—

who could not bear to think of us as
        lost in a nuclear war, dissolved by splitting

atoms as miraculously as they'd conceived us.
        we ate pizza & watched nickelodeon

while they wedged themselves before
        any lawmakers or gods who'd hear

prayers for non-proliferation. that late
        summer afternoon in 1985 they

so believed in their fabric activism—
        thought by unfolding & tying together

each piece they could hug evil
        out of the world & make peace.

oh, mothers of that generation:
        the world is still a vortex of hate.

those men did not listen or act & you
        returned home to trim crusts from bread.

we've grown up & as you'd
        hoped, most were not lost—

but we've seen believing isn't enough.
        blanket the world. blanket as a noun &

verb. cover the earth with your stitchery,
        but the feet always find their way out.

## SITTING ON THE FLOOR IN THE DARK, MY STUDENT ASKS IF WE'VE ALWAYS DONE THIS

~~It is right & proper to begin this~~
~~with a flower — a flower or a bird.~~
~~[Petals & feathers direct us~~
                              ~~how to feel.]~~

Well.

Crocuses were teething, tulips trying out
their legs. Robins shat on rich kids' cars
as comfort cooed through hallways,
groping propped-open doors &
deviants seeking escape to smoke.


[These recollections signal
                              it was spring

           in a very different time.]


Papers tugged at tape binding them to bricks.
Meat patty sweat & tater tot salt
thickened cafeteria air.

          What I want to say is, ~~we were in school.~~ [ah.]

          What I want to say is, ~~it was late April.~~ [oh.]

          What I want to say is, ~~afterwards,~~
          ~~trench coats were banned indefinitely.~~ [hm.]


A year earlier, hunters had pulled an alarm
herding prey into their range. Ninth period
the next day, we had a ~~scheduled~~ fire ~~drill~~.
All looked, none moved toward the door.

But I am ~~thinking too much when I should be~~
feeling [that very statement, a thought].

The lingering of ~~presence~~. The heaviness of
~~want~~. The nearness of ~~our freedom~~. [You expect
       I'll say we could taste it.]


My father visited the restaurant where
I was working an evening shift: *Kids were hanging from windows—
my god, it could have been you.*

  I wondered which end of the gun he meant.

He asked if I'd please come home that night. I spent it
with friends in their basement instead

   & the next

      & the next
& the next.


  Gas dropped down to 95¢ that summer so we drove
  & drove
  & drove
  ~~just to keep moving~~
  ~~to keep up with the moving~~
  to move
  away

& the flowers lost their edges as we passed.

## & I CRINGE EVERY TIME I HEAR THE WORD *WOMB*

To yearn is the sharpest feeling, or is it
to hope? Either way, he fucks as though
he's trying to climb inside my body. To hide
there like he never wanted to be in his
own one in the first place, like he wants
to get back to his mother. I have always
been suspicious of men who cup assured
hands on my belly, willing it to swell with
what's theirs. I can't mate in captivity.
My hands sting & itch. With forehead to
glass I remember three floors is enough
to kill you, but eight is survivable if you have
your mother's flesh to absorb the force.

## ROTATIONAL FALL

> *...a fall where the horse hits a fence with its front legs or chest and its body somersaults over the fence with the fence acting as a pivot point...*
> – equineink.com

in print, witnesses will call this *horrific* without

thinking the word originally meant *to tremble*. you are

halfway in, aware the animal who's carried you is bound

to crush your last breath out of you. bound. if she lives,

she will be aware she killed her keeper. if she dies,

she will have thought it.

good god. it dawns on me how
my sister loved horses so
much more than me, but i ought not
speak of her without knowing her
anymore. i never wore a helmet
but once donned spurs without being
taught how to use them. i held the reins
too tightly: terror was the open pasture,
how the filly let me know
with nostrils flaring
she could take off with me forever.

the saddle a trap, the bridle a death mask

in fragments. as her body lays down onto

yours, you impress your shape into the trembling earth.

## LEGACY

You know the photo: the one of
the young woman with a scarf &
dark hair, crouching over what
used to be a student

screaming *why*

hands plunging into the low atmosphere
as if she can grab her god's shoulders &
shake him for letting this happen.
But you don't know the man in plaid

over her left shoulder. You don't know
his class had been dismissed early to
participate in democracy. He is too far
away & indistinct for you to see the

thick glasses, the mustache he still
wore forty years later. You don't know
that a decade after the National Guard
almost shot him, too, he would become

my father. Daffodils remain silent, but
not complicit: they're still suffering shock.
Flowers planted in gun barrels, tear gas
tossed back at uniforms. Shoots

of yellow flowers from my baptism
poke through early May soil.

# ELEGY WITH APOLOGIES TO LEON JAKOBOVITS JAMES

Six feet away a girl asks do I
        know a term for saying a word
                until it loses ground,
                      becomes a different

thing a bubble on the tongue
        & I am sorry to tell her
                no there is no word in English
                      but in fact there is &

it is *grief*. Five years I've
        driven an automatic yet
                when someone cuts me off
                      I still attempt to downshift & every

night: *I should have called my dad today*
        & then I remember: *oh*.   He is
                a concept, not a thing. This
                      tearing peeling coring like a

placenta detaching after birth
        & I've forgotten the lower half
                of my face. I first learned flirting
                      watching my mother sweat &

call priests their given names,
        most of which meant   *grief*.
                Just because I sense it with my
                      tongue doesn't mean it's flavor. An

exhalation of locusts my babies
    with bones on their outsides & I'd
        rather stab than bludgeon, the blade
            slick and tight. Laughing on

screens, everyone's eyes take dark.
    You, all, organs of mine: watch.
        Halley's comet will return & I want
            to live that long. In my first look

it was a fuzz of light through
    the lens, but it's come into focus now
        as *grief*. I wait like it is the second
            coming of a god I could

lick & grab & this waiting also
    is called *grief*. I'm so desperate
        to find satisfaction that I googled it
            & all the search turned up

was *grief*. Say it over & over with
    ear drums wanting sharper strikes,
        the mouth's musculature fighting free
            as teeth erode to ether.

## OUR LADY OF THE CURIOUS EXEMPTION

consider: over

two millennia of petitions to our lady

coming from men harboring

        contempt for female power.

# STAND HER GROUND

*for Donna Castleberry*

One hundred pounds
        eight bullets
twenty-three years old
        eight bullets
two babies
        eight bullets
eleven thirty AM
        eight bullets
no escape route
        eight bullets
thirty-year veteran
        eight bullets
seventh body
        eight bullets
infinite silence
        eight bullets
the proposition
the trust
the backseat with him on one side &
the door up against a wall on the other
the warrant
        his gun
at home the hungry mouths
        his gun
the child-safe locks
        his gun

his hot breath
        his gun
every man's hot breath
        his gun
not even the scent of cheap air fresheners
the stained upholstery
        his gun
the request
        his gun
memory of steel bars
the plea
        his gun
her self-defense
his reaction
her end
        his gun
any being cornered will fight back
& her teeth already dull from repeated use
        his gun
the history
        his gun
all of history
        his gun
                his gun
his gun
        his gun
        his gun
  his gun
        his gun
    his gun

## FASCINATOR, IN WHICH MOVING ON SERVES AS THE EIGHTH SACRAMENT

here's a catholic guilt poem complete with
daddy verse & i'll mention the moon too
(or is it citrus hung in the sky?) & some birds
flying over an ocean or sea, naturally.
is that blood? on bones? bloody bones in a
mouth sheltering tongue & teeth? note the
softness beneath the tongue, cousin of
dense labyrinths in the inner ear. i ride their
undulations with both my feet in the air.
these will take therapy & sepsis, eclipse
& drought, a whole species' extinction
to shake loose something new. i used to close
my eyes & let another sense lead, not now
that i no longer know the scent of each house.


//


i no longer know the scent of each house
beyond its front door. no, my memory
does not fail—it holds odors in its golden
tabernacle—it is the present tense that
denies olfaction. several bodies i've
held will be dead white men someday. feel
this loneliness, candy canes sucked to points
the year i usurped cold from winter. you

smirk, ask if i've been with another man &
scoff when i say no; you never think to ask
about the women, each another. i have
no right to say so. i think you miss me
even when i'm sitting right next to you,
this hovering skin unable to contain me.


      //


this hovering skin unable to contain me
crepes & folds, each line on the page a new
line on my brow. you killed me waking, then
unearthed me in your sleeplessness: this re-
discovery the last thing i'll ever let you do
to me. you were shit, i a bare foot startled by
your warmth. friend, how did i survive you?
my justified prayers came true: you got
scooped up & thrown in a bin & i,
i live i live i live in your guilt & your
shame & my misfit sainthood fit for a
queen—for a queen's lungs remember the top
& i & my lungs arose arose arose & now
you are the one with arteries exposed.


      //

you are the one with arteries exposed,
scalpel & saw at last opening light.
i thought there'd be photos of me there
but no, just sanguine & shine. as your priest
anoints you i stare down christ with soil caked
on his face, implore it all to *mean* but feel
ice walls slicking the hollows of my chest.
as a child i had faith but it wasn't mine &
i learned not to keep other people's things:
borrow & share, try on & play but never take.
like when a man tries to make me come for
himself not for me at some point I just smile &
push his hand away—no one gets the power
to make me break or pray on command.


      //


to make me break or pray on command
they tried everything: buddy jesus, bully
savior, all the saints i was named for &
our lady of fill-in-the-blank. but who
ever asked if the blank was lacking?
well? oh no, now the moon: even dark
it's still there, nothing need take its place.
my soul lounges barren: no matter how
promising the follicles, my hips won't house
spiritual seed. i savor the attempt
but always evade the implantation & fruition.

too much distraction to grip on, finding
edges too round to keep ahold of. slipping,
here's a catholic guilt poem complete.

# ODE TO THE WORD *VAGINA*

*after Sharon Olds*

More sturdily constructed in the mouth
than the sputter & hiss of *penis*—
nothing flaccid about your labiodental
fricative, the voicing of it rumbling
down to what you name.
No hesitation in the tenseness
of the tongue-muscle between molars
to push the /d₃/ & its spurt of saliva out
into the world from the musty-sweet
root of the throat.
Teeth or no teeth, a monster will taste
its prey, lick it while life sustains
fear. I stand on your legs
screwed into my feet, swat
a winged thing away from my hair.
As the danger-blossom beckons
it from its hive, a single honeybee
can't be accused of swarming.
Your invitation delivers the enchanted
to its trap: the last syllable
proudly grooms her paw.

## OUR LADY OF THE SAFE WORD

remember this
rope burn on your wrists is negotiable:
last time you thought yourself escapeless
you fashioned a knife from your
own shinbone & when it proved too
blunt you slashed a hatch in the plaster
with your tongue & all he saw
was the back of you,
getting smaller.

## HANDS: A CROSS

America? Are you here, were you there? Waiting

in a field halfway to Pittsburgh, my grandma pointed

out Indian Paintbrush—laughed when I asked where

were the painters & what did they paint. I kept these

flowers in my hands so I wouldn't have to hold hers

with their swells of knuckles & slithering veins. At

some point I gave in. At the start so did a girl my age

& I wonder now if this gesture did anything to shush

her rumbling stomach. Are her grown hands like mine,

covered in scars & scales? Does she clasp them in her

lap, sit them on her hips, raise them in the air?

Now the idea that anything could reach all the way

across this country prickles the back of my neck &

the field chokes under asphalt, red petals coughing through.

## UPON FIRST AWARENESS OF CLOUD MOVEMENT, 1985

Maroon handfuls of carpet: coarseness
        mingling in dimpled fingers.
        A faint pressure on the bladder complains.
Through windowpanes doves
        wade in seed hulls
at the base of the feeder
        nodding their heads

to seven inches of hopeful voices
        spinning at 45 RPMs    on shelves built
        of cinderblocks    & two by fours
            & naked need.   *We are the*
    *world. We are the children.*    But the sky
is falling.  Pulling itself    apart    like spiny capsules
splitting around buckeyes.  Like a part lobed    inside of me.
        Can my mother stop this?    Can she
    stop anything?    Yelling in the kitchen.

A shuffle, a bang. *There's a choice*
        *we're making / & it's saving*
        *our own lives.*    I am camouflaging myself
into the floor, holding it & being it.
        I fear I'd fall off    were I not
            holding on    aware of occupying
    a planet    fearing forces
  that move the sky.

## SPELL TO EXTRACT BEAUTY FROM MY MOTHER'S DESPAIR

*When the moon appears full but isn't quite—*
*when it's invisible but you cradle faith*
*it's perched beyond the crackled ceiling—*

        psychologists say memory
        begins around age three, but
        the only system i trust
        is my body's capacity to inherit
        & store. i found this here
        & no one claimed it, so i took
        it in & made a home.
        water-soluble, fat-soluble,
        it makes me & i hold it
        elbow-to-palm like a newborn.

*Gather ransom note clippings from your*
*years-ago journals. Palm the dry bitter rinds*
*protecting wet sweet fruit. Tweeze gravel from*
*your knee-skin & arrange the stones in ovals*
*around a woven-snake rug—*

        desire cringes in embarrassment,
        its chin tilts up—the most
        diamond-like of the scent memories.
        still i mine it behind the latched door
        while dust particles assume i make
        something aromatic or astringent.

*Slather the tongue with bee sting salve.*
*Submit hair to purple flame to cease the*
*bleeding in the brain. Submerge the body*
*under afterbirth of Venus & two*
*eyelids-full of venom—*

        i tilt my head & pour earwax
        into the black hole passing
        through. still, i can't reach my
        thoughts to tell them to shout.
        squatters' rights prevail & her sobs
        tug at the hem of my skirt.

*Steep until the constellations align*
*like lily-of-the-valley. Pat down the embers*
*of your hair & pack the wounds on your knees*
*& hands with leftover ash. Rest*
*your fingertips across your brow.*
*Rest, child. Planets must move slowly,*
*so heavy with their work.*

        she'd have tossed me over a bridge if
        there'd been one nearby. still,
        i stroke her sorrow within me.
        i inebriate it with my milk of forgiveness
        & now it only whimpers while i sleep.

## OBJECTS IN THE ROAD MISTAKEN FOR ANIMALS

last friday, a fast food sleeve hurled
from a car. mid-fall, a crooked branch
      of crisp curled leaves. come spring
a bit of frayed rag, formerly blue.
every mile a wind-animated
grocery bag.    steer into the ditch.
      into oncoming traffic. off the bridge.
I swear I sensed its breath—
      it could have been alive.
           it could have been alive.

## DIGESTIF

Sunlight feeds the forest. A buck stamps,
bobs his antlered head & snorts. I solidify
like gelatin made from his hooves. Decades
have gone since my tongue last pushed meat
against my teeth, yet this is how I end? &
a hawk lay beside the road: wings limp, neck
turned jagged while carrion birds peck past
bent feathers. The news reports nothing left of
the farmer who stepped before hungry hogs,
bucket full of feed ignored as he went down.
In the kitchen my nephew howls & shakes
as I mix cereal with peas. He is all mouth
& no heart. In a bed two hours away
my maker's sparrow bones dissolve to sand.

**II.**

*How will I ever learn to tell the truth*
*After the places my hands have been?*

– Gabrielle Calvocoressi

## ELEGY TOWARD INDIFFERENCE

Fireworks of feathers
trickle like indignant rain &
skyscrapers don't apologize.

Neither does the janitor's
broom as stunned *(but still
alive? still alive)* warblers are

swept up & bagged with
cigarette butts & soda cans.
Glass buildings reflect

trees & sky. After guiding
them trustily across Lake
Erie's breadth overnight

navigation by starlight
is helpless to warn hollow-boned
travelers who've flown over

three thousand miles. On the
eleventh floor, a man pouring
coffee hears a small thump.

Looks to the window, sees
nothing,
stirs in the cream.

## SELF-PORTRAIT AS FAKED ORGASMS

You'd think someone would have checked for a pulse. Turns out no, a body is all they want. The first time: yes, on a bloodstained carpet. The wedding night: yes, almond cake in my hair. The night it happened four times: each time. Elevator, kitchen counter, both times on the roof & I know what you're thinking: why act to make men feel adept? & I am here to tell you: it was not just for the men. I'd learned it was a thing at nine from a Cosmo in a waiting room. Sounded powerful, bright art or light. If now you're wondering *did she ever fake with me?* the answer is yes & I'd apologize but that would be one more. I know someone faked with me long ago & unhurt, I played along. How could I not when her hair smelled of summer spent outdoors? Experts are concerned the internet is teaching everyone performance. The truth is we already know. & by the way, I can only watch porn with the sound turned down because I can't stand all of the faking.

## PARTY GAME

*FUCK:*

Colliding stars swallow each other,
turn inside out & light into lead.
On earth, I catch only shudders
of sense, fold them into my chest
amidst our limbs braiding together.

*MARRY:*

We are hallway footsteps at dawn,
the same floorboard always complaining.
We are terrycloth & cotton batting
against skin, lotioned & shaved.
We are honey-smell bulging into every
corner as bread rises in the oven.

*KILL:*

When you slice & crunch apple flesh
next to me, I know it is time:
the bread burned, the lead poison.
I pitch you to the sky & a new
star holds fruit in its mouth.

## THE DOCTOR WRAPS HER HAND AROUND MY THROAT

& says *swallow. I know, it's odd.*
I swallow. It is odd.
I distract myself by remembering
a flock of swallows is known
as a gulp. A flock of buzzards:
a wake. A murder of crows. Who
assigns the terms that make it so?
A group of beings in a home
is a family. A group of homes:
a block. I heard last week
my old red house has been
painted blue as a bruise (a group
of colors: a palette). It cannot be.
It must be furious red like the myths
fossilized in every beam
(a group of fossils: a dig,
a group of beams: a frame).
Blue is too cool, too assured—
or maybe this is the new owners'
defense. Their refusal to swallow
with its hands around
their throats.
*Good*, she says. *Now again.*

## ON TRYING TO GUESS MY NEWLY-DEAD FATHER'S COMPUTER PASSWORD

| | | | |
|---|---|---|---|
| check under the keyboard | | *because his generation—* | no |
| try: | [his birthdate] | *it multiples: [dd] x [mm] = [yy]* | no |
| try: | [my name + sister's name] | *he liked me more* | no |
| try: | [sister's name + my name] | *or maybe her* | no |
| try: | [his childhood dog's name] | *it's the most common* | no |
| try: | password | *lord, don't let it be* | no |
| try: | buildcommunity | *all he ever wanted to do* | no |
| try: | Bu1ldC0mmun1ty | *but...* | no |
| try: | humanity | *the last thing he asked for* | no |

TWO TRIES REMAIN BEFORE YOUR ACCOUNT WILL BE LOCKED

ARE YOU A ROBOT?   *no*

*:: click on crosswalks ::*

*:: even stray edge-pixels ::*

*i am not a robot*

| | | | |
|---|---|---|---|
| try (oh god): | [my mother's name] | *did he never stop loving her* | no |
| | | *:: exhale ::* | |
| try to try: | [their anniversary] | *& realize I've never known it* | so |
| try: | [name of the sickness that killed him] | | |

YOU HAVE RUN OUT OF TRIES

## MORNING WITH EMPTY CAT DISH

My partner calls it
*still nighttime:*
burrows a hand
into the warmth

of an armpit,
shoulders the combed
flannel quilt higher
under his chin,

floats down
the warm-milk river
of theta waves. I,
though, am already

dressed & have read
the morning's news.
Our gray cat, a
blurred staircase-

zigzag of anticipation
in the dark—she's
excavated her own
reflection in metal

& holds me accountable
for this snub.
*You're ok*, I say & rake
fingernails through

her coat. *The world
won't end.* She storms
my ankles as I open
the can & hold my

breath. Spooning tuna
into the void, I thank
God she's just a cat
so I don't have to lie.

## OUR LADY OF THE FALLOW

Use the phrase *let down* like I know what
it is to cry milk through the front of my

shirt. *Latch* as a closing off or holding in—
depends which side you're on. At forty I switched

to past tense: from I don't have children to
I didn't. It's none of your business, really, but

my ovaries carry such inheritance
they each need a therapist of their own.

In a parking lot I think a seagull is a baby &
go searching for it. Later at home I hear the baby

& think *it's nothing, just a seagull* & scatter
bread scraps on the ground.

## IN WHICH I SUDDENLY RECALL THE FIRST PLANE I SAW IN THE SKY AFTER 9/11

i doubt it saw me coming.
its head never turned in shock
or condemnation. but i saw it.

the bat—its sonar short of
black-salt protection from
impact. from me. for seconds
air pressure held it there & then

it slid away. i cringe
around the echo of bones
clearing skin into glass.
my wipers only widen
the smear.

countless objects in motion, & two are
bound to meet. six days after colleagues
counted to three
& leapt from windows in the sky,
dan rather cried on the late show:
*all those people.*

letterman took his hand & broke
to a commercial. the president told us *go shop*.
i went to bed & dreamed of glass
encasing falling sand.

eyes aimed up to blue, gulls
wailed & at the edge of my view
buildings cowered behind each other.

everyone on the street looked up,
up, up, bound for eventual collision.

# MARRIAGE BORN OF CAUTION

my name a violence
whole body an ear

hearing through fascia
& tendon this skin

freckles & burns
but refuses to blush

& you with your
antler-bone eyes

steer-horn shoulders
you with your twenty-

pound elephant heart
i live in the left

ventricle of it & my
tongue-tip prickles

at what i float on
carry me

to the clearing
your ankles slashed

by crabgrass skin
cells remain

on each blade
still

we graze
never full

## THE NIGHT MY FATHER DIED, I ALMOST BELIEVED IN GOD

funny how I grew up in a cold / house & now i'm scared of it all burning down / flourishes of radiator heat block sunlight / gyrating shadows on the floor prove anger is tangible / a temperature a thing a grabbing of flesh a gathering / of body into one's own / god reverberates between the tops & bottoms of echoes / do you hear me god / is in the echoes / oh / my father feared going to sleep because he might not wake & / then he did so he didn't / now he's up /on the mantle charred crumbs in a vase / walking by i say *hello* or does it sound more like *help* / everything in its place matter holding space / cradling us in unseen swaths / gone / the word ignites behind my tongue before it / can escape i navigate between ghost / shapes blocking my way / lean into the heat / into the heat / in heat / i eat / ie / i find dimension in the sound / weave my fingers throughout / press it to my breastbone / atonement is his i / gave it away said *here i don't need it* / need it / it / iterations of *i love you* unfamiliar like this heat saturate this / room as bent knuckles / melt into waves of / faith of f/aith / of faith

//

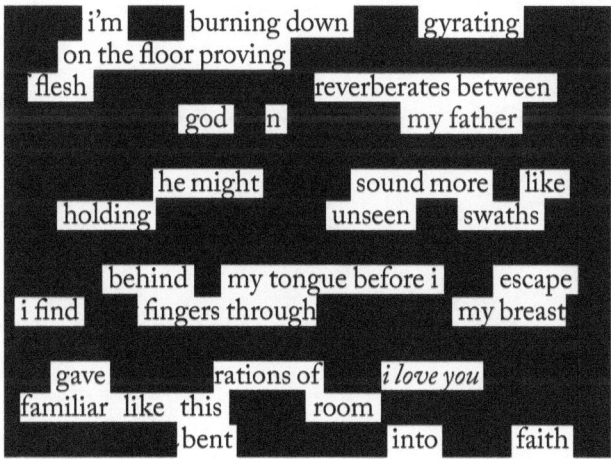

//

flesh berates god her
sound unseen before escape
i find *love* like his

## SHELTER

i have a habit
        of shaking small beings when they
sleep too soundly
& at the top of each stairwell
        I picture my beloveds
        broken at the bottom.
why shouldn't i when
        the woman screaming
                *rape, murder!* in the rolling stones song
        miscarried after the band woke her at 12 AM
            to record that track &
my cousin aimed a gun
through his heart on friday the 13th
        after tripping into love
        & yes, he squeezed the trigger—but only
after muffling the bang with a pillow
to keep from waking his family.
        i'm awake,
a vault of strangers' secrets i've
        vowed to keep muzzled in twine spun
        from the DNA in my baby curls:
            both my grandmothers
        carried pockets full &
            i halt it here.
tell me *you'll change your mind eventually*
        & i laugh as someday leers,
            unrecognizable from miles behind.

## CLEARING MY HISTORY AFTER SEARCHING PLAN B AVAILABILITY IN UTAH
### (because no, this is not what you think)


Call it survival instinct:
in a new place I must taste the air.

Must listen for coyote-throat yips
before toeing the yard, even when I do not

hold rabbit meat. I am writing
like everyone I love is dead,

thus do not consider forgiveness.
You would love for me to have done

What You Thought I Was Doing All Along.
You would love the sniffed trail to yield a kill,

to peel your lips back from canines coated
in thigh fiber. What if: it's been What You've Thought

all along. What would you do then.
I've returned home to find the fanged alpha

dreaming on my pillow,
bloodless snout atwitch.

## OUR LADY OF THE RESTROOM STALL CONFESSIONAL

Now say it: make friction
with your lips & breath.
You already have at the edge
of your mind, now take it
into your mouth.
Open wide, let out stink.
Not how your love grew
a mile a day. None of the
swelling you've felt through
your chest. No stories at all
from your silly red heart—
lying bitch perched amidst
your ribs—this is the place
to let out your shit. What
you need to hear vibrating
each tooth at its root is
how much you would
rather not have this.
How you know you've
been duped & would return
to before. How you hate them
as much as you love &
oh, how you love.

## BODY OF KNOWLEDGE

I will rewrite the dictionary & gift it to everyone I love.

In early childhood, my mother informed me that I had
a *uterus*, that this very special part was a counterpart of the *penis*.

Language: a system of assigning
arbitrary symbols,
feigning standardized meaning.

This system:
used
to mold
understanding
of reality.

>Read: home taught me what makes me female
>is capacity to accommodate.

(She also spoke of *nipples* for feeding babies,
but never whole *breasts* for anything else.)

In elementary school I learned I also had a *vagina*. An escape to the secular
from within my consecrated core.

Centuries of maps
crafted by European men
have misled the world
in understanding itself.

A map:
a definition,
an assignment
of place
& proportion.

>Read: school reinforced that I am to welcome another, to
>fulfill his wishes & needs.

It was not until I found myself unsatisfied by limitation & want that I learned
on my own about the clitoris. My own fingers' ecstatic discovery, later
confirmed at the public library: there was a word for what I'd found. It owned
such a tiny blip on the man-made map of the body that it took
my own expedition to discover.

Any medical professional
will tell you a textbook's
anatomical drawings are mere
approximations.

The body:
more complex
& unruly
than page & ink
can capture.

       Read: pleasure is abundantly available, but no one found this
       important enough to have taught me so.

One more fact, dear reader:
Americans are terrible
at describing gustatory experience,
partially because
our language lacks
adequate words
to articulate flavor.

What other
pleasures
go missing
by not
slathering
their names
onto our hot
tongues?

## ODE TO MY IUD

      1.

*What is this witchcraft?*
Nature asks as I beam
at blood. Our hidden
symbiosis grins. No
parasite depletes me.

      2.

Even the moon is no match:
I am a powerful witch.
Because I love you,
little ones, I will protect you
the only way I know.

      3.

Copper middle finger
aims at old white men
in tailored suits.
Their vision may fail,
but the sign reads clearly:
NO VACANCY HERE.

      4.

Silver lampwork dangles safely
from my earlobes. Devoured
pages retire on shelves; continents
rest ravaged.
Life, sacred after all:
mine.

## THE INSTRUCTOR SAYS BREATHE IN, AS THOUGH I HAVE FORGOTTEN

i tend my body with fullness of yarrow
               spreading teeth      wide
     in a crowded    mouth    the words with
a tongue     untasting of itself
       rooted in pinkness    thin as earlobe skin.

there is no good word for it    but
      what it is.     perhaps my father's
         dishwater voice   perhaps my first
attempt to cry    while the engorged cord
      kept down any sound &

              remnants of berries birthed from dirt

clamped the air.      now four decades gone

where do i send all this   breath holding

     space          in my chest as thistle guards

     the ribcage, woven into each dry bone?

## ON MY FIRST CASE OF CHUB RUB

i am trying to recall what it was to love
hunger. to sit bone-on-bone with it,
edging closer, hoping it would snake
its limbs around me or at least drag a
fingernail across my forearm. i'd covet
its cold scorch near my spine:
sensation with mass
taking up space
echoing back
& forth amid
my ribs—
each rib,
these ribs
&

not that i
felt very guilty
     in the first place, but:
     last time pressure
purpled my
inner thighs
like this
     my teenage lover's
     insistent hips
were to blame
& i wore it
     like a girl
     scout badge.
     a whole
life later,
add stinging
     & a different flavor
     of shame-turned-
pride: it was me
this time. all me.
     i did this. i've fed

                        my body. i listened:
i rested. i grew.
now my thighs

            meet.

                        make themselves
                        known with
rubbing &
sweat &
                        the burn of anything
                        so close.

## AFTER ALL, I PROMISED TO READ ST. AUGUSTINE

True nuns infuse their pious infidelity into
kettles of abortion tea for anyone in need.
My father set out to raise a strong [but not

*too* strong] girl & by now I've scrubbed the enamel
from my teeth. It's all in the elbow, you see? For closure
I need to ask a friend if we ever opened each other up,

but I don't want to rend muscles in his chest again.
Most subway dust is human skin, specks of us crammed
in crevices like the togetherness everyone craves

but few will inconvenience themselves for. Alone
before her curtainless window my neighbor watches
Wheel of Fortune & disrobes to pose for nudes.

I'm confusing *concupiscence* & *cornucopia* again &
might as well indulge. I've thieved at least
a dozen pears but none have led to any god.

## SOMETHING IN

        squid-ink tendrils unfurling
across the firmament
        abruptly as all the gingko
leaves
distance themselves
           from the branch at once

the way obstacles shape
the wind:
        some solid, some mere
pressure pockets

the way these eyes
        didn't used to be the best
feature,
        but now they're all that's
           left

    the way
tooth shards saved
in a jewelry box
        & monarch dust
        shaken from preserved
    wings
both leave behind
        lace skeletons

the way the sky isn't angry

    just working some things out

               the way words are not
owned
      to give or withhold

## SPELL FOR PROTECTION AGAINST THE FORCE YOU CANNOT NAME

*tuesday's child, noon, during
the moon's third quarter.*

*a place that feels safe, meaning
out-of-body. cloves smooth through*

*the nostrils & grate the lungs.
choose three pieces of*

*hematite & into a doll bottle
they go, coated with oil &*

*rolled in coarse salt. see green light
simmer & glow. slide three sprigs*

*of angelica through the neck because
three is half of six. now plug*

*the mouth with calendula pistil
& bind it all in ribbon once,*

*twice, thrice. roll it between your
hands, heel to fingertip to heel*

*& back again. note the hum along
the fate line & the clink, clink, clink.*

*press it between the dangers of your
breasts & think green, green, green.*

*outside your door crouch down to the
ground, down so far if you inhale too*

*deeply the dust creeps in.
rest cheek against earth so*

*bone leans into skin. listen. smell*
*the damp. sit up & scrape a trench in*

*the soil, as deep as you feel the*
*fear. drop in the bottle, kiss it*

*goodbye & hope, hope, hope*
*while covering it in gray stones.*

# ACCIDENTAL ELEGY

Holding your head in my lap
I am terrified        by how easily
I could snap your neck.
    I'm reminded        how I'm not a mother
because any time I cradle
        something smaller than myself
    my hands feel powerful:
not with ill will,        but compulsion to protect.
        To press back the world
gnashing its lichened teeth.
        My hands are of it.
I mold my palm to your crown,
        flatten the wry cowlicks.
    Your temple bone under my thumb
is so thin.        How can it judge danger,
dash away in time?        Your ear cupped
        to my thigh    hears nothing but
    circulating blood.        No warning growl.
No storm siren. I want to lean down,
        but my lips are lined with daggers.
Forgive me if your breath on my knee
    stops mid-sigh. I am made of dust
        from stars
        that do not support life.

# Notes

According to a report from University of Utah researchers in *The Bulletin of the Seismological Society of America* (2019), a rock formation called Castleton Tower does in fact vibrate at approximately the same frequency as a human heartbeat as mentioned in "Self-Portrait with Origin Myth & Orbit."

"To the Women Who Surrounded the Pentagon" refers to an August 4, 1985 project called The Ribbon that took place in Washington, D.C. Participants were encouraged to make fabric panels depicting the theme, "What I cannot bear to think of as lost in a nuclear war."

(CW: Gun violence) Prior to the infamous Columbine school shooting in 1999, the second deadliest school shooting in the U.S. was perpetrated on March 24, 1998 by two Westside Middle School students near Jonesboro, Arkansas. They pulled a fire alarm, then shot at students and teachers as they exited the building. "Sitting On the Floor in the Dark, My Student Asks If We've Always Done This" references both tragedies.

"& I Cringe Every Time I Hear the Word *Womb*": (CW: suicide) On March 13, 2013, a Manhattan lawyer named Cynthia Wachenheim leapt from her eighth story window with her infant son strapped to her chest. She did not survive; her child sustained minor injuries.

"Legacy" refers to a Pulitzer-winning photograph taken at Kent State University on May 4, 1970 by John Filo of Mary Ann Vecchio kneeling over the body of Jeffrey Miller.

Dr. Leon Jakobovits James coined the phrase "semantic satiation" in his 1962 doctoral dissertation at McGill University. It is a psychological phenomenon in which a repeated word or phrase temporarily loses meaning for the speaker or listener.

"Stand Her Ground" is for Donna Castleberry, a sex worker who in August of 2018 was trapped in the backseat of a car by a Columbus, Ohio undercover police officer who shot her eight times at close range after she attempted to defend herself from him.

The third sonnet in "Fascinator, in Which Moving On Serves as the Eighth Sacrament" is after the poem "rose" by Danez Smith, which was first published at *Homology Lit* and later included in their poetry collection *Homie*.

"Fascinator" is simply my term for five sonnets linked together in the style of a longer crown or half-crown of sonnets.

Hands Across America took place on May 25, 1986 as a benefit for the organization USA for Africa.

"Upon First Awareness of Cloud Movement" borrows its italicized lines from the popular 1980s musical collaboration "We Are the World," which was written by Michael Jackson and Lionel Richie.

"Elegy Toward Indifference" takes inspiration from the Cleveland Plain Dealer article "Good Samaritans rescue hundreds of stricken songbirds from downtown sidewalks" by James F. McCarthy, which ran on September 29, 2017.

The phrase "cry milk" in the first sentence of "Our Lady of the Fallow" takes inspiration from a section of Heather Christle's *The Crying Book*.

"In Which I Suddenly Recall the First Plane I Saw In the Sky After 9/11" refers to my own recollection of an episode of The Late Show that aired nationally on CBS on September 17, 2001. A recent reviewing of this episode reveals that my memory paraphrases what Dan Rather actually said, but the descriptions of his and David Letterman's actions are accurate.

The "twenty-pound elephant heart" in "Marriage Born of Caution" is reminiscent of a line from the poem "How to Triumph Like a Girl" by Ada Limón.

"The Night My Father Died, I Almost Believed in God" is in the form of a burning haibun, which was invented by torrin a. greathouse.

The title "Shelter" is a reference to the Rolling Stones song "Gimme Shelter."

"Spell for Protection against the Force You Cannot Name" takes inspiration from Arin Murphy-Hiscock's book *Spellcrafting*.

# Acknowledgments

The following journals have published or will be publishing poems (sometimes in slightly different forms) in this manuscript:

*Cherry Tree*: "Clearing My History After Searching Plan B Availability in Utah (because no, this is not what you think)"

*Cream City Review*: "personal sonnet while hail accumulates, no 6" (which appears in this manuscript as the second section of "Fascinator, in Which Moving On Serves as the Eighth Sacrament")

*Dialogist*: "Self-Portrait as Faked Orgasms"

*Entropy*: "Elegy Toward Indifference"

*Glass: A Journal of Poetry*: "Our Lady of the Safe Word"

*Gordon Square Review*: "To the Women Who Surrounded the Pentagon"

*Grist*: "Our Lady of the Fallow, I Cringe Every Time I Hear the Word *Womb*" and "After All, I Promised I'd Read St. Augustine"

*Jelly Bucket*: "Spell to Extract Beauty from My Mother's Despair"

*Kissing Dynamite*: "Party Game"

*Longleaf Review*: "Stand Her Ground"

*Lunch Ticket (Amuse-Bouche)*: "On Trying to Guess My Newly-Dead Father's Computer Password"

*Noble/Gas Qtrly*: "Our Lady of Impermanence"

*Palette Poetry*: "Ode to the Word *Vagina*"

*Pigeonholes*: "Our Lady of the Restroom Stall Confessional"

*Pleiades*: "Sitting On the Floor in the Dark, My Student Asks If We've Always Done This"

*Rabbit Catastrophe Review*: "Objects in the Road Mistaken for Animals"

*Split Rock Review*: "Digestif"

*Sundog Lit*: "The Night My Father Died, I Almost Believed in God"

*The Academy of American Poets (Poets.org)*: "Legacy"

*The Boiler*: "Rotational Fall"

*West Branch*: "Elegy with Apologies to Leon Jacobovits James"

*wildness*: "Self-Portrait with Origin Myth and Orbit"

# Thank You

I want to express profound gratitude to the following persons and programs. Without their guidance, advice, support, and encouragement, this book would not exist:

George Abraham, Kaveh Akbar, Leila Chatti, Ada Limón, José Olivarez, and Solmaz Sharif for leading incredible workshops with wisdom, patience, high standards, and honest constructive feedback. My workshop-mates, too: you know who you are, and I love you all. Jericho Brown, Taylor Byas, Camille Dungy, Ross Gay, Terrance Hayes, Aimee Nezhukumatathil, Maya C. Popa, and Nancy Reddy for inspiring craft talks and Q&A sessions that motivated me in much-needed ways. Geramee Hensley & Jeremiah Ockunzzi, for writerly companionship and all-hours critiques large and small. Kaleigh O'Keefe & Josh Savory, for early belief in and enduring support of my work. torrin a. greathouse, for generous and candid feedback on a few of these poems. Eloisa Amezcua, for generative prompts, feedback, and helping me get unstuck. Steve Healey for selecting this work as the winner of the Trio Award; Tayve Neese, Matt Mauch, Hadley Hendrix, and everyone else at Trio House Press for guiding me through the editing and publication process.

The Kenyon Review Writer's Workshop and Minnesota Northwoods Writing Conference for organizing vibrant and productive writing communities, and the National Writing Project at Kent State University for reinforcing from the beginning that K-12 teachers have a professional and moral obligation to write. The Speakeasy Project and 24 Pearl Street for running generative workshops that resulted in many of these poems. The people I've met through each of these organizations have been instrumental in my development as a writer.

My parents and sister for nurturing a love of words from the beginning. Katie Dysert. The Hortons in their many iterations, and the Wolfpack. Andrea Alexander. Oscar, Violet, and Nito. And, of course, Chris—for everything.

**About the Author**

Megan Neville (she/her) is a writer and educator based in Cleveland, Ohio. She is the author of the chapbook Rust Belt Love Song (Game Over Books, 2019). She is a National Board Certified Teacher of English Language Arts in Adolescence/Young Adulthood, and holds BSE and MEd degrees from Kent State University. She was the winner of the 2019 Wick Poetry Center Contest for Peace & Transformation, and has been a finalist or semifinalist for the Write Bloody Book Contest, the Akron Poetry Prize, the Frost Place Chapbook Contest, the Tupelo Press Sunken Garden Chapbook Contest, and the YesYes Books 2020 Open Reading Period, and others.

## About the Artist

Erin McGean studied Fine Art at York University in Toronto and although originally trained in painting and drawing, she has been producing analog and digital collages for over 10 years. Erins work explores themes of motherhood and femininity through the repurposing of vintage found imagery. Her work can be found in corporate and private collections throughout Canada and the USA. Born in St. Catharines and raised in Mississauga, Erin currently resides in Oakville, raising her family, teaching high school visual arts and practicing her craft.

# About the Book

*The Fallow* was designed at Trio House Press through the collaboration of:

Tayve Neese, Lead Editor
Hadley Hendrix and Natasha Kane, Supporting Editors
Joel W. Coggins, Cover Design
Erin McGean, Cover Art
Hadley Hendrix, Interior Design

The text is set in Adobe Caslon Pro.

The publication of this book is made possible, whole or in part, by the generous support of the following individuals or agencies:

Anonymous

# About the Press

**Trio House Press** is an independent literary press publishing three or more collections of poems annually. Our mission is to promote poetry as a literary art enhancing culture and the human experience. We offer two annual poetry awards: the Trio Award for First or Second Book for emerging poets and the Louise Bogan Award for Artistic Merit and Excellence for a book of poems contributing in an innovative and distinct way to poetry. We reserve the right to select other titles to publish from contest submissions.

Trio House Press adheres to and supports all ethical standards and guidelines outlined by the CLMP.

**Trio House Press, Inc.** is dedicated to the promotion of poetry as literary art, which enhances the human experience and its culture. We contribute in an innovative and distinct way to poetry by publishing emerging and established poets, providing educational materials, and fostering the artistic process of writing poetry. For further information, or to consider making a donation to Trio House Press, please visit us online at www.triohousepress.org.

Other Trio House Press books you might enjoy:

*Bloomer* by Jessica Hincapie

*Unceded Land* by Issam Zineh

*Sweet Beast* by Gabriella R. Tallmadge / 2021

*The Traditional Feel of the Ballroom* by Hannah Rebecca Gamble / 2021

*Third Winter in Our Second Country* by Andres Rojas / 2021

*Songbox* by Kirk Wilson / 2020 Trio Award Winner selected by Malena Mörling

YOU DO NOT HAVE TO BE GOOD by Madeleine Barnes / 2020

*X-Rays and Other Landscapes* by Kyle McCord / 2019

*Threed, This Road Not Damascus* by Tamara J. Madison / 2019

*My Afmerica* by Artress Bethany White / 2018 Trio Award Winner selected by Sun Yung Shin

*Waiting for the Week to Burn* by Michele Battiste / 2018 Louise Bogan Award Winner selected by Jeff Friedman

*Cleave* by Pamel Johnson Parker / 2018 Trio Award Winner selected by Jennifer Barber

*Two Towns Over* by Darren C. Demaree / 2018 Louise Bogan Award Winner selected by Campbell McGrath

*Bird-Brain* by Matt Mauch / 2017

*Dark Tussock Moth* by Mary Cisper / 2016 Trio Award Winner selected by Bhisham Bherwani

*The Short Drive Home* by Joe Osterhaus / 2016 Louise Bogan Award Winner selected by Chard DeNoird

*Break the Habit* by Tara Betts / 2016

*Bone Music* by Stephen Cramer / 2015 Louise Bogan Award Winner selected by Kimiko Hahn

*Rigging a Chevy into a Time Machine and Other Ways to Escape a Plague* by Carolyn Hembree / 2015 Trio Award Winner Selected by Neil Shepard

*Magpies in the Valley of Oleanders* by Kyle McCord / 2015

*Your Immaculate Heart* by Annmarie O'Connell / 2015

*The Alchemy of My Mortal Form* by Sandy Longhorn / 2014 Louise Bogan Award Winner selected by Peter Campion

*What the Night Numbered* by Bradford Tice / 2014 Trio Award Winner selected by Carol Frost

*Flight of August* by Lawrence Eby / 2013 Louise Bogan Award Winner selected by Joan Houlihan

*The Consolations* by John W. Evans / 2013 Trio Award Winner selected by Mihaela Moscaliuc

*Fellow Odd Fellow* by Stephen Riel / 2013

*Clay* by David Groff / 2012 Louise Bogan Award Winner selected by Michael Waters

*Gold Passage* by Iris Jamahl Dunkle / 2012 Trio Award Winner selected by Ross Gay

*If You're Lucky Is a Theory of Mine* by Matt Mauch / 2012

www.ingramcontent.com/pod-product-compliance
Lightning Source LLC
Chambersburg PA
CBHW030346100526
44592CB00010B/840